To: Dear Ian,

With love &
Best Wishes for your
Birthday

From: Grandma & Grandad.
x x x x

200H

# AUSTRALIA

# BEAUTIFUL
# AUSTRALIA
## IN PICTURES

PHOTOGRAPHS BY GEOFF HIGGINS

TEXT BY DALYS NEWMAN

WOOLLAHRA

# INTRODUCTION

Vast, ancient and unique, Australia is the world's smallest continent and largest island, a land of contrast and contradiction. Landform varies dramatically from the sparkling, vibrantly coloured wonders of the Great Barrier Reef to steaming, lush rainforests of northern Queensland, through an endless coastline of rugged, eroded formations and surf-pounded golden beaches, to snow-sculpted alpine forests, barren deserts and glittering gibberstone plains.

With shores washed by three oceans and four seas and an area of nearly 800 million hectares, the diversity of scenery, climate and vegetation is immense.

Australia is the driest continent on earth but in parts of it the average rainfall exceeds 375 centimetres. It is the flattest continent, but its mountains, from the blazing red domes and pinnacles of the MacDonnell Ranges in the Northern Territory to the snow-capped peaks of south-western Tasmania are scenically magnificent. Two-fifths of the continent lie north of the Tropic of Capricorn. But a tropical vista in Australia may be one of parched treeless plains even more frequently than it is of palm-fringed beaches, jungle-covered mountains or coral islets.

These assorted habitats, along with the country's isolation and geographical antiquity have led to a vast and unique assortment of flora and fauna. Over 120 different species of marsupial animals are native to the continent and nearly 90 per cent of Australia's plants are found nowhere else in the world. No wonder early settlers were alarmed by the baby animals that found refuge in their mother's pouches, the strange furry creatures that lived in

BELOW: Mackenzie Falls in the Grampians National Park, Victoria. ENDPAPERS: Sand dunes in the Gibson Desert, Western Australia. HALF-TITLE: Sunset at Crowdy Bay National Park, New South Wales.

rivers and laid eggs like birds and the trees that shed their bark instead of leaves. Much of this natural heritage has been preserved and protected from encroaching civilisation in the many national parks and wilderness areas that contain a wealth of wildlife, scenery and serenity.

Australian people and places are equally multifarious. From sleepy former gold-mining towns to vast cattle stations, palm-fringed international resorts, dust-streaked country towns, the chrome and glass of skyscraper studded cities and bustling commercial centres, there is a place for everyone to find a lifestyle of one's own. The fierce arid red heart of the continent has forced an adherence to the coast—over 80 per cent of the population find refuge in urban areas on the coastal strip, separated by the Great Dividing Range from the strange and powerful wilderness of the Australian outback. Even the people who inhabit this vast land are unique. A truly multicultural society, over 2 million migrants from more than thirty countries have brought their history and culture to enrich this young nation.

First settled on 26 January 1788, when Captain Arthur Phillip, first governor of the colony, along with some 1487 convicts, civilians and soldiers, landed at Sydney Cove, Australia has a simple, uncomplicated history. Early days of convict settlement, intrepid explorers battling their way into the remote interior, a booming sheep industry and the discovery of gold have all made their mark on the country—along with the rich cultural heritage and ancient art forms of the Aboriginal people.

With a land so contradictory and diverse there is much to discover and enjoy. It is a country for everyone.

PAGES 2 AND 3: Koonchera Sand Dune on the Birdsville Track, South Australia. TITLE PAGE: Windmill at Sunset, Barradine, New South Wales. PAGE 8: The Amphitheatre, Finke Gorge National Park, Western Australia

# CONTENTS

# NEW SOUTH WALES

New South Wales is the most populated and dominant state in the Commonwealth of Australia, containing more than a third of the land's people. It is a state of contrasts, home of Australia's largest city, incorporating extremes of country ranging from sub-tropical to alpine and covering an area of 801 428 square kilometres.

It is also the country's founding state. Named New South Wales by Captain James Cook in 1770 when he took possession for the British of all Australian territory east of the 135th meridian of east longitude, the state has since shrunk somewhat and occupies just 10 per cent of the continent. It was first established as a penal colony in 1788, transportation continuing until 1840.

Many country towns reflect the state's past: relics of the early gold and agricultural history of the rich central tableland and plains region are found in and around towns such as Dubbo, Bathurst and Wagga, and the nostalgic river boat era is immortalised in the Murray River towns.

The state naturally divides into four regions: the narrow, fertile coastal lowlands; the sparsely populated western plains, which take up two-thirds of the state; the high tablelands and peaks of the Great Dividing Range and the pastoral and farming country of the Range's western slopes.

Within these regions can be found mountain, lake, river and forest scenery of memorable beauty, breathtaking coastlines, irresistible golden beaches, autumn-coloured high mountain vistas and the frontier territory of the state's extreme north and west.

The exciting cosmopolitan city of Sydney, set on the world's most beautiful harbour, offers all the cultural, commercial, sporting, gourmet and entertainment diversions you would expect from a great metropolis. Despite this variety and sophistication, sunshine, a welcoming sea and a relaxed outdoor lifestyle make up the essence of the city. Remnants of Sydney's past integrate with the gleaming towers, colourful crowds and snarling traffic. Old pubs, bandstands, sandstone cottages and terrace houses are a testament to colonial days. Sydneysiders are proud of their city: it is the cradle of Australian history and industrially and commercially, the focal point of the South Pacific.

Of all the Australians states New South Wales has, arguably, the greatest variety of interests to offer the visitor—the lively and sophisticated city of Sydney, many hundreds of kilometres of glorious ocean beaches, magnificent river, lake and mountain scenery and the harsh, fascinating emptiness of the interior.

LEFT: Australian icon and one of the world's best known pieces of modern architecture—the Sydney Opera House. ABOVE: Darling Harbour, Sydney's playground, a spectacular recreational and commercial centre created in a former shipping and storage area for the Port of Sydney. ABOVE RIGHT: The endearing koala—at home in the eucalypts.

ABOVE: Sunset spotlights Fort Denison, originally built to protect Sydney from the Russian fleet cruising the Pacific during the Crimean War, but the predicted attack never came. It was later used to house recalcitrant prisoners who were kept on short rations and the island became known as 'Pinchgut'.

LEFT: City lights at night—the Sydney CBD skyline seen from Darling Harbour.

RIGHT: Boating, fishing and all watersports are popular on the large expanse of Brisbane Water stretching from the coast inland to Gosford, about 80 kilometres north of Sydney.

LEFT: Wind-patterned sand at Mungo National Park in central western New South Wales. Up until 25 000 years ago Lake Mungo had 10 m deep water and tree-lined banks, yet today it is totally dry and covered with scrub. It is also the site of the oldest known human occupation in Australia

BELOW: Dusk descends on Mungo National Park.

RIGHT: Thrills and spills of white water rafting on the Nymboida River in north-eastern New South Wales.

OVERLEAF: The Harbour Bridge bursts into fiery colour during the dramatic annual New Year's Eve fireworks display on Sydney Harbour. Over 20 000 fireworks, let off from barges in the harbour, light up Sydney's skyline on this spectacular occasion.

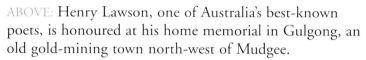

ABOVE: Henry Lawson, one of Australia's best-known poets, is honoured at his home memorial in Gulgong, an old gold-mining town north-west of Mudgee.

ABOVE RIGHT: All aboard for the Zig Zag Railway at Lithgow. Built in 1868, this breathtaking stretch of railway was regarded as an engineering masterpiece in its time. The track was gradually rebuilt during the 1970s and 1980s, mainly by volunteer workers who

also acquired historic rolling stock from all over Australia.

BELOW: Reflective solitude on Willandra Creek in Willandra National Park, habitat of many waterbirds.

RIGHT: Ebor Falls, one of the attractions of Guy Fawkes River National Park, noted for its wilderness scenery, rugged river, rapids, gorges and mobs of kangaroos.

ABOVE: Bushwalkers enjoy the panoramic view from Crater Bluff in the Warrumbungle National Park, on the western slopes of the Great Dividing Range near the town of Coonabarabran.

LEFT: The Needles, one of several huge granite tors studding the landscape of the Gibraltar Range National Park situated on a high escarpment at the eastern edge of the New England plateau.

BELOW: The Central Business District of Broken Hill. An oasis in the arid wastelands of far western New South Wales, the town was created to serve the miners in the rich silver-lead zinc deposits of the Barrier Range.

ABOVE: Heavy rains play havoc with outback roads at Tibooburra, a former gold town north of Broken Hill. The far west of New South Wales is harsh, forbidding territory—running out of petrol, food or water can literally become a matter of life and death.

LEFT: Fields of wheat near Young in the western foothills of the Great Dividing Range. Wheat growing is one of the major agricultural activities in New South Wales and more than 1000 new varieties have been developed to suit Australian conditions.

PREVIOUS PAGES: Sturt National Park—the most remote of the state's parks—is a true outback experience with open deserts, gibber plains, endless red sand dunes, flat-topped rocky mesas, lakes and billabongs.

BELOW: The Australia Telescope sits like a giant frilled neck lizard 20 kilometres west of the cotton-producing town of Narrabri in north-eastern New South Wales.

ABOVE: Snow sculptures herald wintertime at Kosciuszko National Park in the heart of the Snowy Mountains.

LEFT: The Thredbo River splashes through Kosciuszko National Park. This park embraces a large area of the continent's only extensive alpine region, including the nation's largest snowfields.

BELOW LEFT: Woven wares at the Brown Shutter, Berrima, an unique historic village south-west of Sydney. Founded in 1829, the village has hardly changed over time and is an important part of Australia's heritage.

OPPOSITE TOP: A diversity of coastal land-forms—headlands, cliffs, wave-cut platforms and small off-shore stacks—line the 27–kilometre shoreline of Murramarang National Park.

OPPOSITE BOTTOM LEFT: The convict-built Sea Horse Inn, still functioning as a licensed inn, is one of the few buildings in Boydtown, formerly a rival settlement to Eden.

OPPOSITE BOTTOM RIGHT: Australia's oldest commercial wine-producing area, the Hunter Valley is dotted with vineyards producing red and white table wines ranking among the best in the country.

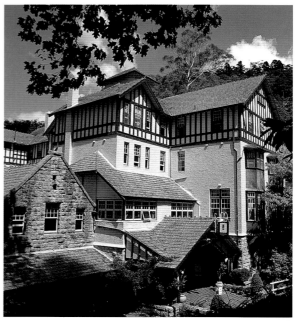

ABOVE: Soft browns and greys intensify to fiery rich golds and reds as sunlight touches Hanging Rock in the Blue Mountains.

RIGHT: Wentworth Falls tumble into a verdant valley in the Blue Mountains National Park.

PREVIOUS PAGES: Forever inseparable, the Three Sisters stand sentinel over the spectacular scenery of the Blue Mountains. Here, high precipices rise from densely wooded valleys and deep gorges making much of the terrain inaccessible except to skilled bushwalkers and mountaineers.

OPPOSITE TOP: Cascades in the upper reaches of Barrington Tops National Park where six major rivers spring into life. A remarkable range of natural habitats occur in this park, from alpine plateaus to steaming rainforests.

OPPOSITE BOTTOM LEFT: Autumn tones at Mt Wilson in the Blue Mountains. English-style gardens, filled with bulbs and deciduous trees, thrive in the cooler climate of this area.

OPPOSITE BOTTOM RIGHT: Rest a while at the old-world Caves House after exploring the remarkable underground limestone caves and above-ground arches of the Jenolan Caves.

ABOVE: The General Grocer and Produce Store at Hill End. Formerly a bustling gold-mining town with a population of 30 000, the now sleepy hamlet has been proclaimed a national historic village.

RIGHT: Sunset over the coast at Hat Head National Park. Surfing and fishing are favourite activities in this north-eastern New South Wales park.

BELOW: Formerly known as The Granites, the old gold town of Tibooburra is surrounded by granite outcrops. The town's name comes from the Aboriginal word meaning 'heaps of boulders'.

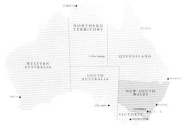

# AUSTRALIAN CAPITAL TERRITORY

Heart of the nation, the Australian Capital Territory is comprised of two tracts of land: 23 200 hectares on the shores of Jervis Bay near Nowra, New South Wales and 235 000 hectares of highland on the western slopes of the Great Dividing Range south-west of Goulburn, New South Wales. The area has an indefinable quality of spaciousness and grace, enhanced by the beautiful Mongolo River valley and surrounding hills, mountains and pastureland.

The Australian Capital Territory was created out of New South Wales territory by an Act of Parliament on 1 January 1911 after a great deal of controversy and several sites being chosen. Before this the area was mostly farmland. Rather than site the Federal Parliament at an existing city the new Federation preferred a purpose built capital for the government of the nation. It wasn't until 1927 that the parliament actually sat for the first time in its new home when it was opened by the Duke and Duchess of York on 9 May. Prior to that the Australian Parliament sat in Melbourne.

The fine natural port of Jervis Bay has never been developed commercially—it was transferred from New South Wales to the Australian Capital Territory in order to give the Federal Capital sea access.

The country's capital, Canberra is central to the Australian Capital Territory. Set on an undulating plain in an amphitheatre of the Australian Alps, it was conceived and developed as the seat of national government and administration. It is also a centre for learning and the arts—a showplace and a symbol of Australian creative talents.

One of the world's best-known fully planned cities, Canberra was designed by American architect Walter Burley Griffin who won the international competition for the city plan in 1912. His concept was for a garden city with a series of lakes and a great triangle of avenues enclosing the government buildings, with Parliament House on Capitol Hill the central viewpoint of the city.

Concentric circular streets, planted with more than four million native and exotic trees and shrubs, are set graciously on the shores of the man-made Lake Burley Griffin. Cosmopolitan restaurants and the international flavour of diplomatic missions introduce an interesting ambience to the city. Impressive public buildings have turned the city into a gleaming showplace and draw visitors from throughout the country.

Canberra's architecture and atmosphere is unique and stimulating, it is a city of rare beauty and spectacular progress.

---

LEFT: Evening light colours Canberra's impressive High Court building, opened by Queen Elizabeth II in May 1980. ABOVE: The Australian National Library houses an extensive collection of books and documents including Captain Cook's journal. INSET: Australia's most famous ambassador—the kangaroo.

ABOVE: The 53 bells of the Carillon, a three-column bell tower given to Australia by the British Government to mark Canberra's half-century, echo over the shores of Lake Burley Griffin.

ABOVE LEFT: Reaching for the skies, the large dish-shaped antenna at the Tidbinbilla Deep Space Tracking Station receives information from craft exploring the deep reaches of the solar system.

LEFT: Floodlighting enhances the flowing Grecian lines of the Australian National Library, which stands on the southern shores of man-made Lake Burley Griffin.

RIGHT: Fortunes are to be made and lost at the imposing Casino Canberra.

PREVIOUS PAGES: Hot air balloons make safe landings on the tranquil waters of Lake Burley Griffin. In the background, the Telecommunications Tower rises 195.2 metres above ground level on the summit of Black Mountain.

RIGHT: Visitors from throughout Australia make a pilgrimage to enjoy the bountiful delights of the Floriade, the country's most stunning floral display.

BELOW: Autumn tones in Canberra. Tree-planting has always been important in this city as the site was not abundantly endowed with natural bushland due to extremes of climate.

OVERLEAF: The heart of the nation—Parliament House on Capitol Hill. Designed by Aldo Giurgola, and costing nearly one billion dollars, it was officially opened in 1988. Its magnificent 81–metre stainless steel flagpole dominates Canberra's skyline.

LEFT: Blundell's Farmhouse, built in 1858 by the Campbells of Duntroon for their ploughman, has been furnished with pieces contemporary to the district's early history.

OPPOSITE: Cascading Gibraltar Falls are located south-west of the capital

BELOW: One of Canberra's most famous attractions, the model English village of Cockington Green is a draw-card for young and old, containing scale models of British buildings such as Braemar Castle, inns and cottages.

# QUEENSLAND

Queensland, the Sunshine State, is evocative of endless summers, tropical islands set in jewel blue seas and eternal holidays. It is the second largest state in Australia and just over half of it lies north of the Tropic of Capricorn.

Geographically, the state comprises four main regions which all run north to south; the tourist resort-studded coastal strip, Australia's premier playground; the lushly vegetated mountain system of the Great Dividing Range; undulating, sparsely timbered tablelands, crisscrossed by slow, meandering rivers and the flat, hot, semi-arid plains of the Great Artesian Basin.

This rich variation of Queensland's scenery is preserved in its national parks which offer endless stretches of shimmering sands and pounding surf, a coast of coral reef and great dune systems, and inland areas of rugged ranges, high waterfalls, cloud-shrouded rainforests and tropical flora and fauna.

The relaxed, easy-going city of Brisbane is Australia's third largest. Straddling the Brisbane River, and sprawling over a small series of hills, it is filled with lush parks and gardens brimming with sub-tropical plants. Brisbane is growing rapidly and is tipped to become Australia's second largest city in the next century. The two main centres of the tropical northern region are Townsville and Cairns, the latter an excellent base for the exploration of the surrounding lush sugarlands, mountainous jungle country and wilds of Cape York Peninsula. Port Douglas, a little north of Cairns has become a playground for international visitors and has been developed as a resort during the last twenty years.

The Great Barrier Reef, the world's largest and most famous coral formation, stretches down the coast, sheltering the many beautiful resort islands which lie off the coast. With over 700 islands dotted through the sparkling azure sea, and the banks of coral reefs shadowing the water, this sun-drenched tropical paradise is unique.

The colourful, exuberant stretch of the Gold Coast is the most intensively developed and highly publicised holiday area in Australia. Surfers Paradise, with its raging night life and golden, surf-pounded sands is undoubtedly the brightest star along the 30 odd kilometres of beaches, relaxation and development.

Queensland's mild, sunny climate, its exciting city centres with their casinos and nightclubs, its beautiful mountains and reef-fringed tropical coast attract visitors from all over the world.

LEFT: Frothing waves and glistening golden sands make the fully patrolled Surfers Paradise beach a favourite haunt for surf 'n' sun enthusiasts. TOP: Skyscrapers at Main Beach on the Gold Coast are reflected in the waters of the Nerang River. INSET: The colourful King Parrot.

ABOVE: The classical lines of Brisbane's Anzac Memorial contrast with the towering modern architecture of the city centre.

RIGHT: Night descends and Brisbane, the relaxed, easy-going capital of Queensland, lights up. Australia's third largest city, Brisbane was named after the Governor of New South Wales, Sir Thomas Brisbane.

BELOW: Mount Isa, where silver-lead, copper and zinc are mined, is the most important commercial, industrial and administrative centre in north-west Queensland.

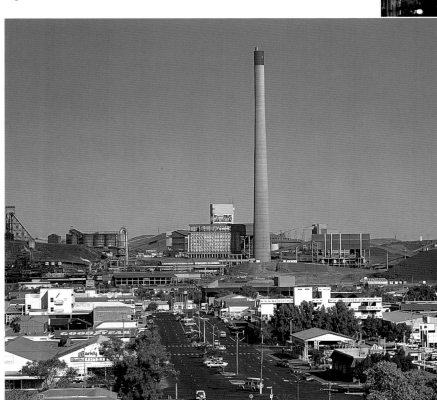

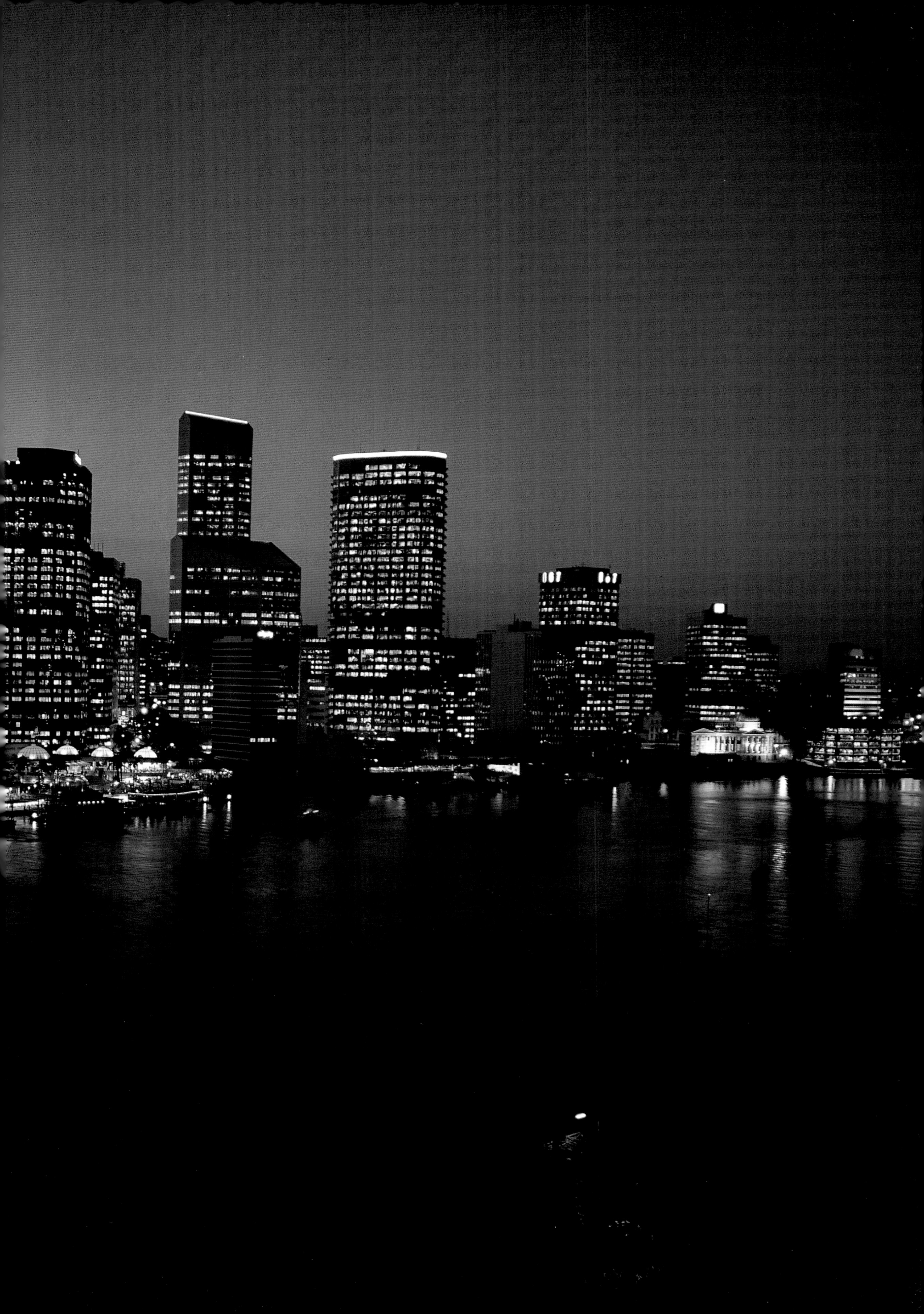

ABOVE: Sheer limestone outcrops, resembling the battlements of ancient towers, and an extensive underground cave system are protected in the Chillagoe-Mungana Caves National Park, west of Cairns.

LEFT: White sandstone cliffs, canyons, gorges and narrow ravines are the distinctive features of the 28 500–hectare Carnarvon National Park, one of the most breathtakingly scenic reserves in Australia.

BELOW: The Chimneys, a striking rock formation in Carnarvon National Park.

OVERLEAF: Rugged, lunar-like landscapes create dramatic effects in inland Queensland, west of Winton.

ABOVE: Mist slants through rainforest that stretches from mountain tops to sandy shores at Cape Tribulation, north of Cairns. A number of rare, primitive flowering plants can be found in this area.

RIGHT: Elebana Falls, one of more than 500 waterfalls plunging into the gorges and valleys through dense rainforest vegetation in Lamington National Park in south-eastern Queensland.

OPPOSITE TOP RIGHT: The Eliot Falls crash into the Jardine River, the largest perennial stream in Queensland. Jardine River National Park is situated in the tropical wilderness of Cape York Peninsula.

OPPOSITE BOTTOM LEFT: The wreck of the Maheno is one of several ship's carcasses embedded in the shallows of Fraser Island, the largest island off Queensland's coast and the largest sand island in the world.

OPPOSITE BOTTOM RIGHT: Crocodiles, the most ancient and majestic survivors of the reptile epoch, are one of the most fear-inspiring animals in Australia today. There are 2 species, the ferocious saltwater crocodile and the less aggressive freshwater species.

PREVIOUS PAGES: Porcupine Gorge near Hughenden in Central Queensland. Hughenden is about the halfway point between Charters Towers and Cloncurry.

OPPOSITE: Zillie Falls, near Millaa Millaa, on the Atherton Tableland. Once wild, remote and almost entirely covered with rainforest, this area is now mostly cleared and dotted with farmhouses.

LEFT: Waterfalls and rock formations create a dramatic setting at the 200–hectare Natural Arch National Park, south of Brisbane.

BELOW: After the northern monsoons the rivers of Queensland's far-west and south-west corner flood through the countryside, renewing life and filling waterholes.

RIGHT: Lady Elliot Island, a sparkling coral cay off Queensland's coast, caters to Great Barrier Reef visitors with glass-bottomed boats, reef-walking, snorkelling and scuba diving.

OPPOSITE: Sun sets on the tip of Cape York. The peninsula is a sanctuary for most of Australia's unique wildlife, including crocodiles, orchids and insect-eating pitcher plants.

BELOW: Sparkling sand-fringed bushland of Moreton Island, a remarkable wilderness island only 35 kilometres east of Brisbane. Apart from rocky headlands, the island is mostly sand hills, native scrub, banksias and freshwater lakes.

OVERLEAF: Tatts Hotel at the town Winton, where the Stockman's Hall of Fame can be found.

OPPOSITE: Precariously perched, the Sphinx is a granite rock formation in Girraween National Park, high on the Great Dividing Range.

OPPOSITE BOTTOM: Cane harvesting—sugar growing is a major industry in northern Queensland. First brought to Australia from South Africa in 1788, large-scale cultivation began near Brisbane in 1864 and the industry spread rapidly up the coast.

OPPOSITE BOTTOM RIGHT: Preparing for corroboree, Cape York.

ABOVE: Creeks flow through tangled rainforest on Fraser Island. This unique area of freshwater lakes and dense rainforests attracts abundant bird and animal life.

RIGHT AND OVERLEAF: Canoeing on Lawn Hill Creek which snakes its way through the Constance Range in Lawn Hill National Park, a remote oasis in the dry plains of northern Queensland.

ABOVE: Marlin Wharf, Cairns, from where the rich, famous and otherwise leave to do battle with giant black marlin from September to December each year.

LEFT: The Endeavour River winds through Cooktown, the site where Captain James Cook beached the Endeavour in 1770 to repair damage after running aground on a coral reef.

RIGHT: Sailing at Shute Harbour, launching pad for exploring the 100 or so tropical islands of the beautiful Whitsunday waters.

PREVIOUS PAGES: A peaceful scene on the Gregory River north of Mt Isa.

OPPOSITE: The century-old Birdsville Hotel is the ideal rest stop for tourists travelling down the infamous Birdsville Track into South Australia.

LEFT: Roadtrains thunder along the dry, dusty, endless roads of the outback.

BELOW: Saltpans near Burketown in Queensland's Gulf Country. Often flooding, this area can be isolated for long periods during the 'Big Wet', generally from November to April.

OVERLEAF: The verdantly framed Millaa Millaa Falls in the Atherton Tablelands.

# VICTORIA

Victoria, the Garden State, although the smallest state on the Australian mainland is the second most densely populated and productive with industries including coal, the oil rigs of Bass Strait and fields of natural gas. Woven into these activities is a strong rural heritage. Rich soils, extensive grasslands and perfect rainfall provide ideal ingredients for sheep and cattle grazing, vineyards and other crops.

Framed by the Murray River, the ocean and the South Australian border, Victoria has a chequered landscape of noble mountain ranges and forest. Small neat towns and large prosperous cities contrast with rivers winding through gentle green valleys while the rugged coastline has a wild and haunting beauty.

Each of Victoria's five main geographical regions has its own special attraction. Sleepy, faded goldrush towns and the Grampians, the state's most beautiful natural garden, dominate the central and western districts. The western district south of these ranges offers rich grazing land dotted with splendid old homesteads and the spectacular scenery of the Great Ocean Road. While the north-east alpine region is crowned by the gently rounded peaks of the Victorian Alps stretching endlessly under clear skies.

The Gippsland region contains beautiful and varied countryside with inland waterways, the Ninety Mile Beach and many national parks.

Settled by Scottish and English immigrants and lacking the rough and tumble convict beginnings of New South Wales, it is a gracious state, with many well-preserved reminders of its heyday during the gold rush of the late nineteenth century. The sophisticated and charming city of Melbourne, with its wide tree-shaded streets and elegant Victorian buildings contrasting strongly with modern tower blocks, has an unruffled elegance and style all of its own. A truly cosmopolitan city, it is a place of bustling markets, delicatessens and restaurants, swanky boutiques and clanging trams.

From its earliest beginnings Victoria has blended beauty and productivity—the early settlers created a solid foundation of economic strength and planted a multitude of gardens as they moved throughout the colony.

These elements are still paramount in the Victoria of today—the state retains an air of hardworking industriousness, while doing much to cultivate the arts and conserve its magnificent architectural heritage.

---

LEFT: Tourist boats on the Yarra River, symbol of the spirit of Melbourne. ABOVE: The Melbourne skyline and night lights on the banks of the Yarra. Centred on the north bank of the river, the city, Australia's second largest, has an unique unruffled style and elegance. INSET: The raucous laughter of the Kookaburra is heard in both suburbia and bushland.

ABOVE, LEFT: The city skyline with the Daimaru building in the foreground.

CENTRE, LEFT: Pleasure craft anchor off St Kilda beach, near the head of Port Philip Bay. Once a small village, St Kilda was named by Superintendent La Trobe in 1842.

LEFT: Flinders Street Railway Station, Melbourne, deals with the daily rush of suburban train travellers.

ABOVE RIGHT: One of Melbourne's fleet of modern trams passes the Princess Theatre.

RIGHT: Sleek concrete and glass giants, interspersed with mellow historic buildings—Melbourne's skyline seen from the footbridge over the Yarra.

OPPOSITE: Riotous colour at the Botanic Gardens—one of several peaceful retreats for city-dwellers created throughout Melbourne. Many of the majestic old oaks in the garden are over 100 years old.

LEFT: The eternal flame burns brightly outside the imposing, pyramid-shaped Shrine of Remembrance in Kings Domain, Melbourne.

BELOW: Sunset frames the pier at St Kilda. Once Melbourne's leading seaside playground, this cosmopolitan spot throngs with life at weekends.

OVERLEAF: Newly ploughed fields at Hopetoun, a small mallee town just south of Wyperfield National Park.

OPPOSITE: Granite peaks, sweeping white beaches, steep headlands, tall forests, fern gullies, salt marshes and abundant wildlife are found in Wilsons Promontory National Park, on the southernmost tip of Australia's mainland.

LEFT: At Tidal Creek, near the main camping site in Wilsons Promontory National Park, the water is stained a muddy brown from tannin derived from decaying plant matter.

BELOW: Steep granite headlands fall to sheltered bays and white beaches at Wilsons Promontory National Park.

RIGHT: Erskine Falls cascade through mossy boulders in the scenic Otway Ranges behind the tiny coastal resort of Lorne.

OPPOSITE: Warm temperate rainforest, spring wildflowers and walking trails are features of Lind National Park in East Gippsland.

BELOW: Boroka Lookout affords a bird's eye view over the Grampians, a series of high weathered ridges forming the westernmost heights of the Great Dividing Range.

OVERLEAF Early morning mists shroud the granite cliffs and frothing Crystal Brook Falls in Mount Buffalo National Park.

ABOVE: Enduring rural reminders at Kiewa Valley, Tallangatta. The old town of Tallangatta was submerged due to construction of the Hume Weir, but many of its buildings were moved to a higher, new location.

RIGHT: The *Emmylou* paddlewheeler plies her way through Echuca. Once Australia's largest inland port, it has now been restored to the period of its heyday.

OPPOSITE TOP: Elegant homes, built in the traditional English style were much favoured in the nineteenth century by those living in the inner Melbourne area.

OPPOSITE BOTTOM LEFT: Many of the attractive buildings in the former gold-mining boom town of Chiltern have been classified by the National Trust.

OPPOSITE BOTTOM RIGHT: Bright township, an attractive tourist centre and base for winter sports enthusiasts at the foothills of the Victorian Alps.

ABOVE: A thin sliver of sand dunes separates the ocean from the Gippsland Lakes, which form the largest network of inland waterways in Australia. Lakes Entrance is the main resort town at the mouth of the lakes.

LEFT: Sunset over Mallacoota Inlet. This picturesque area offers the beautiful, remote countryside of the Alfred, Lind and Croajingolong National Parks to explore.

BELOW: Petrified forest at Cape Bridgewater near Portland.

OVERLEAF: Sunset at the Twelve Apostles, renowned natural sculptures formed by the seas pounding the limestone plateau around Port Campbell on Victoria's south coast.

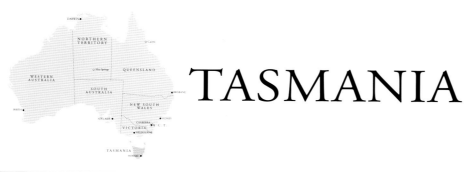

# TASMANIA

Tasmania, the wettest and the smallest of Australian states, has some of the most magnificent scenery in the country, with several areas being World Heritage listed. Almost seven per cent of the area has been set aside for national parks, providing Australia's best rafting areas and most celebrated systems of mountain and ocean walking trails.

The world's most mountainous island, Tasmania's landscape is very different from that of the mainland—nowhere is one out of sight of distant jagged mountain peaks, ranges or green, lushly forested hills. Surrounded by the treacherous waters of Bass Strait, the Southern Ocean and the Tasman Sea, and buffeted by cold southerly winds, it has a wild, wet and rugged reputation, softened by arcadian pastures and compact greenery. Scenic delights range from the incomparable wildness of the west coast, great inland lakes feeding savage rivers, the towering mountains of the central district, the gentle pastoral landscapes of the midlands, the lush orchard country around Launceston and on the Huon Peninsula to the snug bays, beaches and villages of the east coast.

Tasmania's convict past is preserved in the grim ruins of the Port Arthur settlement. For nearly fifty years Van Diemen's Land, as it was then known, was a brutal penal colony, home to 67 000 convicts. More European in style than the mainland, the enchanting countryside is dotted with huge old English trees, stately homes, mellow farm houses, old oast houses and many quaint historic villages. Everywhere one is reminded of the wealthy and the damned of Tasmania's past.

Hobart, the state's capital, is built around a beautiful yacht-studded harbour at the foot of the majestic Mt Wellington. Once a lusty, brawling whaling port, the city today has a gentle European air with its colonial sandstone buildings, snow-capped winter backdrop and thriving waterfront. Because of the ready availability of suitable timber from the Tasmanian forests and its coastal setting Hobart became involved in the ship-building industry in the nineteenth century, making it an important port. This heritage is still evident today.

To the north of Hobart are several beautifully preserved nineteenth century villages such as Richmond, Ross, Oatlands and Campbell Town.

Tasmania is an island of contradictions. Of incomparable true wilderness areas and gently tamed farmlands. Of churches and pretty historic towns and the reminders of the stark brutality of convict days.

---

LEFT: Liffey Falls, near Deloraine in northern Tasmania. ABOVE: Richmond Bridge, spanning the Coal River, is Australia's oldest bridge. It was built by convicts between 1823 and 1825 and is said to be haunted by their cruel overseer. INSET: The Tasmanian Devil, Australia's largest marsupial predator.

ABOVE: Wrest Point Casino, Australia's first hotel/casino, is Hobart's star attraction.

OPPOSITE: The gunpowder mill is part of the Penny Royal Watermill complex, one of Launceston's most popular tourist attractions, which includes a museum, working cornmill and a windmill.

OPPOSITE, RIGHT: Sandy Bay, Hobart, is the site of the University of Tasmania, one of the oldest established universities in Australia.

RIGHT: Colourful bustle and bargains galore at the Salamanca Markets in Salamanca Place, Hobart. This sympathetically restored area displays the finest row of early merchant warehouses in Australia.

OPPOSITE: Fishing boats at Bridport, on the north-east coast. Fine beaches and excellent sea, lake and river fishing make this a popular holiday resort.

RIGHT: Cattle graze on rolling green fields at Beulah in northern Tasmania. The state's economy depends heavily on agriculture and related pursuits.

BELOW: The quaint little village of Stanley nestles under a brooding rocky outcrop known as The Nut. The town was the birthplace of Australia's only Tasmanian prime minister, the Hon. J.A. Lyons (1932–1939).

OVERLEAF: The icy peaks of Cradle Mountain are reflected in the waters of Lake Dove in the Cradle Mountain—Lake St. Clair National Park, the most famous natureland in north-western Tasmania.

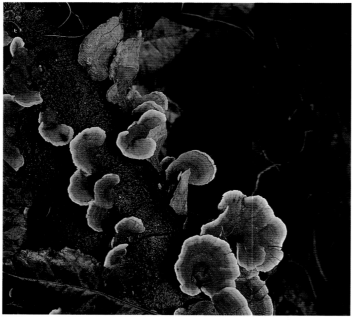

OPPOSITE TOP: Alpine scenery in western Tasmania.

OPPOSITE BOTTOM LEFT: Golden-edged fungi give a fairyland feel to the forest. In these damp rainforest habitats a beautiful array of fungi can be found growing in profusion on the soft decaying wood of fallen logs, trees and the rich, moist forest floor.

OPPOSITE BOTTOM RIGHT: Bleak and forbidding, the Devil's Gullet, Great Western Tiers. A thick layer of dolomite makes up this vast escarpment in central northern Tasmania.

LEFT: Wintertime on Cradle Mountain. The national park has been classified as a World Heritage area and comprises one of the last great temperate wilderness areas in the world.

BELOW: Late afternoon light colours the rugged dolomite-capped Cradle Mountain. The jagged peaks of this mountain tower over small lakes set into its ice-carved hollows.

OPPOSITE: Hogarth Falls, near Strahan, the only town on Tasmania's forbidding west coast.

LEFT: Scotts Peak Dam is one of three camping areas around Lake Pedder in the Southwest National Park, a World Heritage classified area.

BELOW: Rest stop for bushwalkers overlooking the picturesque Wineglass Bay in Freycinet National Park on the island's east coast.

RIGHT: Slightly more substantial than
the signposts of today—a milestone
at Nile near the historic village of
Evandale. This area abounds with
historic interest—nearby Clarendon
House is probably Australia's grandest
Georgian mansion.

BELOW: Bushwalkers enjoy the
varied plant communities around
Lake St Clair in the Cradle Mountain-
Lake St Clair National Park. The
lake, discovered in 1826, occupies a
basin gouged out by two glaciers more
than 20 000 years ago.

OPPOSITE: Electric lighting throws the
stalagmites and stalactites of King
Solomon Cave into spectacular relief.
This fine limestone cave is one of
two situated west of Mole Creek in
northern Tasmania.

PREVIOUS PAGES: The Hazzards, a red granite mountain range, tower over Coles Bay. This beautiful unspoilt bay on the Freycinet Peninsula is known for its abundant birdlife and flora, including more than 60 varieties of small ground orchids.

ABOVE: The Tasman Peninsula extends from the Forestier Peninsula south-east of Hobart, screening Pitt Water and the Derwent estuary from the Tasman sea.

RIGHT: Set like a great mirror among the surrounding ranges of Southwest National Park, the man-made Lake Pedder reflects the moods of storms and sunsets.

BELOW: Magnificent mountain, bush and coastal country in Southwest National Park covers 442 240 hectares, the largest wilderness area in Tasmania.

LEFT: Road to Queenstown—carved out of the surrounding mountains and affording one of the most spectacular views on any highway in Australia.

ABOVE: Enjoy a comfortable walk through stunning rainforest at Arve Falls near Geeveston in southern Tasmania.

BELOW: The sun slowly sinks over Norfolk Bay on the Tasman Peninsula.

OVERLEAF: Tasmania's extensive cool temperate rainforests provide charming vistas. Because of the high annual rainfall evenly distributed all year round, forest of this type is widespread and thick, found at all altitudes from sea level to about 1300 metres.

OPPOSITE TOP: Sight-seeing launches make regular trips up the mouth of the Gordon River, one of the state's largest and more remote waterways.

OPPOSITE BOTTOM LEFT: Quaint old cottages such as Anne's Old Rectory, give the attractive fishing port of Dover an old-world atmosphere. The town was once a convict station and the original commandant's office still stands.

OPPOSITE BOTTOM RIGHT: Jetting down the Derwent River near New Norfolk.

ABOVE: Port Arthur's many-spired historic church was said to have been designed by the convict James Blackburn. In bleak weather the ruins reflect the feeling of hopelessness and misery which existed there about 130 years ago.

RIGHT: The Guard Tower at the Port Arthur Historic Site on the Tasman Peninsula. Once a notorious penal settlement, the ruins are now the greatest single tourist attraction in Tasmania. An unwelcome addition to the grim history of Port Arthur was Australia's worst massacre in 1996 when 32 people were killed by mass-murderer Martin Bryant.

# SOUTH AUSTRALIA

Half of South Australia consists of desert, a world of mesas, sand dunes, salt lakes and temperature extremes. It is the driest state in the driest continent with 83 per cent of the land receiving an annual rainfall of less than 250 mm.

These vast, harsh, northern inland areas have mostly been left well alone by South Australia's population who congregate in the cool productive south of the state. Here, in the fertile Clare and Barossa valleys some of Australia's finest grapes are grown, and further east, in the Murray Valley, citrus of all kinds thrives. The mighty Murray River completes its journey at Lake Alexandrina and historic river-crossing towns still bear traces of the riverboat days.

The area around the state capital, Adelaide, is the most picturesque in the region. Here, the Adelaide Hills shelter tiny villages with magnificent homes, restaurants and craft shops. Adelaide itself is a gracious, well-planned city set on a narrow coastal plain between the rolling hills of the Mount Lofty Ranges and the sparkling blue waters of St Vincent's Gulf. Known as the 'city of churches', it is a spacious, elegant city, well-endowed with greenery and home to a biennial arts festival of international repute.

South of the city, idyllic sandy beaches stretch to the wild, beautiful tip of the Fleurieu Peninsula at Cape Jervis. Modern development has barely touched this area, nor the adjacent Kangaroo Island, a magical combination of sun and sea, native flora and fauna.

There is a profusion of wildlife in the state's national parks. Nowhere else in Australia can be seen so many species in such close proximity. To protect these animals and their habitats, 5 per cent of the state has been set aside as national, conservation and recreation parks. Wild surf beaches, swamplands, rippling sand dunes, high forested ranges and the red soils, white ghost gums and blue skies of the Flinders Ranges are the scenic highlights of the region's naturelands.

Initial settlement of South Australia was the result of one man's ideas of how to create a modern colony. Edward Gibbon Wakefield put his theories into practice in 1836 in the Gulf St Vincent area. The first settlers landed on Kangaroo Island, then Surveyor-General Colonel William Light established a settlement at what is now Glenelg but these sites were soon abandoned in favour of the site occupied by Adelaide today.

South Australia is a land of genteel, cultured people, a land of grace and wine. It is also a place where tough opal miners live underground to escape the searing heat and only two dusty tracks—the Birdsville and Strzelecki—traverse the desert wastelands.

LEFT: P.S. *Mundoo* plies the Murray River at Goolwa, once a key port in the golden days of the riverboats. ABOVE: Coober Pedy, in the heart of the Australian outback, is the country's opal mining centre. INSET: The large, prehistoric lace monitor, an arboreal lizard that grows to a length of 2 metres.

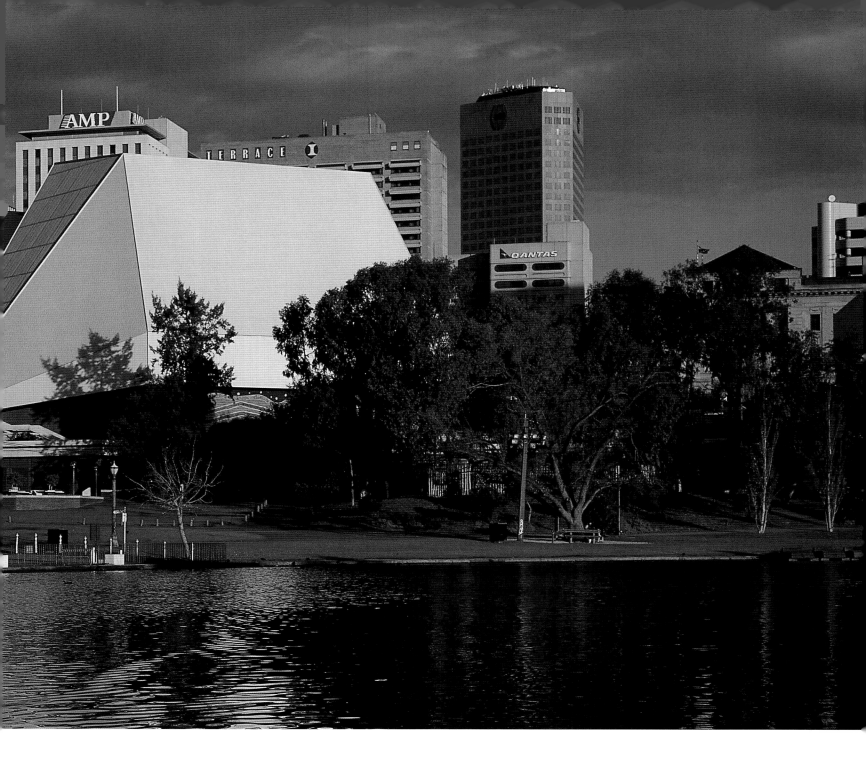

ABOVE: Adelaide's Festival Theatre, a hive of
activity every two years when the city stages its
Festival of Arts featuring world-renowned guests
and leading orchestras and drama companies
from throughout the nation.

OPPOSITE BOTTOM LEFT: Chateau Dorien, one
of the many wineries in the Barossa Valley,
Australia's most famous wine producing area.
About 60 per cent of the nation's best wine is
produced in this region.

OPPOSITE BOTTOM RIGHT: Charming old
towns and vineyards set out in precise, well-
tended rows give the Barossa Valley a distinctly
European atmosphere.

RIGHT: A cornucopia of colourful produce spills
from a street stall in Rundle Mall, in the heart of
Adelaide's bustling shopping complex.

RIGHT: A houseboat wends its way up the Murray River, Australia's 'Old Man River', rising in the Australian Alps and flowing west and south for 2600 kilometres to join the sea at Lake Alexandrina in South Australia.

OPPOSITE: A colourful horse drawn tram on a pier at Victor Harbour in Encounter Bay.

BELOW: Burra, a former copper mining centre, is dotted with many relics of its boom period when over 2000 people lived here.

OVERLEAF: An old homestead now used as a film set in the Flinders Ranges National Park. Abandoned stone farmhouses are a common sight throughout South Australia, standing as stark reminders of the harshness of Australian rural life.

OPPOSITE TOP: Wind patterned and sculpted—the Merty Merty sand dunes. The subtle designs of desert dunes can be found all over the northern two-thirds of South Australia.

OPPOSITE BOTTOM LEFT: Danger at Coober Pedy. Some of the opal veins are 30 metres below the ground and large shafts are sunk into layers of sandstone to reach them.

OPPOSITE BOTTOM RIGHT: Large mounds of dirt, the result of opal diggings, scatter the landscape at Coober Pedy.

LEFT: Patchwork paddocks of farmland near Goolwa. South Australia's economy is basically agrarian, with most of the cropped area in wheat, barley and oats.

BELOW: A disused railway station at Oodnadatta, a tiny outback town that was a busy depot in the 1870s when the overland telegraph line was being built.

OPPOSITE: The picturesque old Cape du Couedic Lighthouse, one of the landmarks on Kangaroo Island.

LEFT: Sunning sea lions at Seal Bay, Kangaroo Island. These creatures were virtually wiped out by sealers but have recently returned to the island where they are now protected.

BELOW: Camel ride at Victor Harbour, a popular resort town and unofficial capital of the Fleurieu Peninsula. Camels were introduced into the country by Afghan traders who drove their camel trains into the outback in the 1800s.

RIGHT: Desolate, harsh countryside around Coober Pedy. Severe temperatures, often reaching 54°C, have forced the population underground—most people here live in dug-outs. The town was originally called the Stuart Range Opal Field because of its location in the barren Stuart Range.

OPPPOSITE: Sunset silhouettes the Casneaux Tree in the Flinders Ranges. The tree was first photographed in 1937 by Harold Casneaux, famous photographer of the Australian Pictorial Movement.

BELOW: The intricately etched peaks of Warren Gorge in the Flinders Ranges had their origins in ancient foldings of the earth's crust, followed by ages of erosion.

OVERLEAF: Ochre-toned, unforgiving country at Lyndhurst where the Strzelecki Track, a harsh dusty 494–kilometre road to Innamincka, has its origins.

ABOVE: The Remarkable Rocks, a group of huge granite boulders weathered into curiously smooth shapes in the Flinders Chase National Park, Kangaroo Island.

RIGHT: Geological history can be read in the many-coloured horizons of the unbroken cliffs bordering the edge of the Nullarbor Plain on the Great Australian Bight.

BELOW: The sun goes down on Cape de Couedic lighthouse. With its sandy beaches, stunning scenery and protected wildlife, Kangaroo Island is a popular family holiday destination.

ABOVE: Drilling for oil in South Australia. The state's areas of the Eromanga and Cooper Basins form a major portion of Australia's onshore oil fields.

LEFT: Outback railway—old tracks of the original 'Ghan' train, replacing Afghan camel drivers on the route from Adelaide to Alice Springs.

BELOW: Going nowhere—pre-loved property, reminder of hopes and dreams at the Waukaringa homestead ruins 30 kilometres north of Yunta.

ABOVE: Dry stony land and richly lined rock faces, contrasting with lush vegetation are distinctive characteristics of the rugged natural wilderness area of the Gammon Ranges National Park.

OPPOSITE TOP: According to Aboriginal legend, Dreamtime serpent Arkaroo carved out gorges and riverbeds near Arkaroola as he slithered his way to drink from nearby lakes. Here, quartzite razorback ridges rise over elongated valleys, once the sea bed of a great continental shelf.

PREVIOUS PAGES: Mood indigo over the Spencer Gulf at Whyalla, an important industrial centre and port.

OPPOSITE BOTTOM LEFT AND RIGHT : Seas and winds have sculpted a dramatically exposed foreshore at Hallet Cove. Eroded rock formations at Hallet Cove, south of Adelaide.

RIGHT: Chambers Gorge, one of several beautiful gorges cutting through the northern section of the rugged Flinders Ranges which extend almost 800 kilometres inland from St Vincent's Gulf.

# WESTERN AUSTRALIA

Covering nearly one-third of the continent, Western Australia is the country's largest state. Most of the area is harsh, vast uninhabitable desert and the majority of the population cling to the coastal areas.

Topographically, the state can be divided into three regions, the Great Plateau, dotted with hills, peaks and ranges, remnants of ancient erosion, which makes up about 90 per cent of the land surface, the coastal plain and the scarplands in between them. Climate varies dramatically within these regions from the damp, temperate Southern Ocean coast to the intense heat of the far north.

It is a state immensely rich in minerals, where intrepid miners battle the searing heat to extract iron ore and other precious metals from the ancient rocks of the desert. The Pilbara region, in the far north-west of the state is one of the most heavily mineralised areas in the world and the biggest exporter of iron ore.

Landscapes of iron-red ranges, spinifex, gaping gorges, gum-lined river beds, wild-flower rich sandplains, forests of towering karri, bold granite headlands and endless stretches of lonely white beaches are contained in the diverse National Parks of this region. Spectacular wildflower displays are perhaps the best known feature of these magnificent parks.

The site for Perth had been visited in 1697 by the Dutch mariner de Vlamingh, who named the Swan River after the black swans he had seen there.

Settlement of the west occurred in about 1826 when south-coast Albany was founded by a party sent from New South Wales. The capital of Western Australia, Perth was founded three years later by Captain James Stirling and though it is the first non-convict settlement in the country some convict labour was used between 1850 and 1868. Many of Perth's early public buildings were constructed in this period. Perth is a charming, modern city on the banks of the Swan River. Easy going and friendly, the city has beautiful beaches and a near perfect climate—it is Australia's sunniest capital.

Western Australia is a unique, separate state. To reach it from the south-east one must cross the treeless expanse of the Nullabor and from the north one must skirt the edge of the great sandy desert from Broome to Port Hedland. It is truly the last frontier of a frontier nation. This isolation is perhaps best illustrated by the many species of flora and fauna that are found nowhere else on the Australian continent. Over 7000 species of wildflowers bloom here and animals such as the marsupial quokka and the termite-eating numbat are unique to the state.

---

LEFT: Boab trees are a common sight in the Kimberley region. Native to drought-prone areas, these trees have the ability to store water in their trunks. ABOVE: Intrepid four-wheel-drivers take a break in the heart of the Gibson Desert. INSET: The dingo was brought to Australia by the Aborigines at least 5000 years ago.

ABOVE: Kings Park offers a panoramic view over Perth and the graceful Swan River. First settled in 1829, Perth is a big country town at heart, home to less than a million people.

LEFT: London Court, an Elizabethan style arcade in the centre of Perth. The city's many multi-storey buildings blend attractively with its colonial architecture.

FAR LEFT: Vibrant floral displays in the 404–hectare Kings Park, set aside as parkland in 1831 by the colony's first surveyor-general, John Septimus Roe.

RIGHT: The bright lights of Burswood Casino, reflected in the waters of the Swan River.

OPPOSITE: Ancient, dwarfed shrubs struggle for a toe-hold in the intensely red rock of the rugged, barren Kennedy Ranges.

LEFT: The mighty 800–kilometre long Murchison River has carved deep gorges and winding valleys out of coastal sandstone in Kalbarri National Park. After heavy rains the normally placid river is a muddy brown torrent.

BELOW: Lake Argyle, the largest man-made lake in Australia, was created by the Ord River Dam and holds nine times the volume of water of Sydney Harbour.

OPPOSITE: Ancient mountains, high plateaus, rivers and deep gorges are features of the Karijini National Park. Hamersley Range slopes gently up from the south to flat-topped outcrops and in the north rises majestically from golden spinifex plains.

LEFT: Lush riverine vegetation, beautifully sculptured cliffs and deep permanent waters where the Fitzroy River cuts through Geikie Gorge in the Kimberleys. The bleached area marks the high-water line of the river in the wet season.

BELOW: Sheer rock walls drop to deep, tranquil water at Yardie Creek, Cape Range National Park.

OVERLEAF: The golden limestone Pinnacles, formed by sand and wind erosion in the Nambung National Park, were mistaken by seventeenth century Dutch seafarers for the ruins of an ancient city.

RIGHT: The vagaries of nature have created strangely eroded formations, such as 'London Bridge' at the town of Sandstone, about 500 kilometres inland from Kalbarri.

OPPOSITE: Friable sandstone rock has been weathered into exotic shapes and interesting bands of colour in the Kalbarri National Park. The cream, brown and vivid red sandstone in this area is called 'tumblagooda'.

BELOW: Stunning bold, granite coastal scenery at Two People Bay, east of Albany.

ABOVE: A pearling lugger at Streeters Wharf, Broome. Their heyday is over but some luggers still fish for young pearl oysters to supply stock for cultured pearl farms nearby.

RIGHT: Yardie Creek, the only permanent water in the rugged Cape Range National Park, flows to the Indian Ocean through a deep gorge hewn out of sedimentary rock.

BELOW: Sociable bottle-nose dolphins regularly come in to frolic with visitors at Monkey Mia, Shark Bay, offering a unique opportunity to make contact with these magical sea creatures.

ABOVE: Formations of unique, multi-coloured jasper gave the town of Marble Bar its name.

LEFT: Sun gilds the perfect curves of Walga Rock, near Cue, a former gold-boom town north-east of Perth.

BELOW: The natural quartz outcrop of the China Wall shines whitely in the unrelenting sun near Halls Creek, on the northern fringes of the Great Sandy Desert.

PREVIOUS PAGES: Wave-battered cliffs and headlands, caves and fantastic rock formations are features of the Geographe Bay and Leeuwin-Naturaliste National Park.

OPPOSITE TOP: Eagle Point near Denham, the most westerly town in Australia.

OPPOSITE BOTTOM LEFT: Time out at the pub at Marble Bar, reputedly the hottest place in Australia, with temperatures regularly exceeding 38°C.

OPPOSITE BOTTOM RIGHT: Walk back in time through the tropical timber buildings of Chinatown in Broome, once a boisterous centre of the pearling industry.

LEFT: Vast amounts of iron ore are extracted from open-cut mines in and around the towns of Newman and Tom Price.

BELOW: Night lights on a mine site at Kalgoorlie, still a prosperous gold mining centre, producing 70 per cent of the gold mined in Australia.

OVERLEAF: The Bungle Bungles, one of the wonders of outback Australia, are a series of gigantic sandstone towers formed over 350 million years ago.

# NORTHERN TERRITORY

The Northern Territory, comprising one-sixth of the Australian continent, is the realm of the real outback. Known as the 'dead heart' or 'the centre' of Australia, it is a sparsely populated area stretching from the centre of the continent to the northern coastline. Distances are vast and scenery is extreme, influenced by both the effects of too much water or of too little.

The remorseless regime of monsoon and drought has created an unique environment in the Top End, by the shores of the Timor and Arafura seas. Here, crocodiles swim in muddy estuaries, heavy vegetation clothes low-lying coastal plains, wide billabongs are covered with lilies, clouds of geese circle clear blue skies, waterfalls plunge down spectacular cliff formations into fascinating river canyons, colourful wildlife roams lush tropical forests and rocks and caves reveal a wealth of ancient Aboriginal rock paintings. Here, too, is the eight million hectares of the Arnhem Land Aboriginal Reserve, one of the country's most fascinating wilderness areas.

Further south, lack of water colours the landscape. Here is the arid desert outback and the shimmering colours of the Red Centre, awesome natural wonders such as the ancient great dome of Uluru and other places of great spiritual meaning to the Aboriginal people. The unique harsh beauty of the outback is here in all its glory with rugged rocky ranges and sun-scorched vistas of red rock, golden spinifex, ghostly gums and deep blue skies. The colourful cliffs of the quartzite MacDonnells arc across the central landscape, cut by deep canyons and gorges. Flat featureless desert landscape stretches as far as the eye can see, occasionally broken by ranges, hills, gorges and isolated outcrops. It is a landscape of many geological wonders.

The Northern Territory's two main centres are more than 1500 kilometres apart. Darwin, at the Top end, is a relaxed, casual city, rebuilt after the devastation of Cyclone Tracy in 1974. It is one of Australia's most multicultural settlements, embracing people of 47 different racial and cultural backgrounds. Darwin Harbour was discovered in 1839 by Lt John Lort Stokes of HMS *Beagle* and who named the area after the naturalist Charles Darwin.

Alice Springs, in the heart of the Red Centre, grew up around an Overland Telegraph Station. It is a thriving tourist centre and is the gateway to the Territory's biggest scenic attraction, Uluru.

Harsh, unpredictable and extraordinarily magnificent, the Northern Territory is a region of breathtaking beauty. It is a timeless land whose people still battle the elements of nature.

LEFT: Ghost gums, eerie guardians of Palm Valley in the Finke Gorge National Park. ABOVE: Sunset over one of the many shallow lagoons and billabongs which attract thousands of waterbirds and magpie geese to Kakadu National Park. INSET: The jabiru forages in the swamps and grasslands of northern Australia.

**ABOVE:**
Torrential annual flooding of the Katherine River has cut a mighty gorge through rock plateau leaving ancient sandstone walls towering above the waterway.

**LEFT:** Sculptures by William Ricketts, depicting the Aboriginal Dreamtime, are featured at the Pitchi Ritchi open-air pioneer museum and bird and flower sanctuary at Alice Springs.

**RIGHT:** Alice Spring's Old Telegraph Station, for many years the only reason for the existence of a handful of people in this remote area. Operating for over 60 years, it now contains a display of memorabilia relating to the early settlement.

**OVERLEAF:** Rising high above the desert plain, the twenty-eight great rock domes of Katatjuta are venerated by the Aborigines as 'the many-headed one'.

LEFT: Undulating floodplains, the cracked and craggy Arnhem Land escarpment and an outstanding concentration of Aboriginal art make the Kakadu National Park one of the country's most magnificent natural reserves.

RIGHT: Steep and stark, the 5-metre wide walls of Stanley Chasm, a spectacular cleft in the MacDonnell Ranges, west of Alice Springs.

BELOW: Golden light bathes Rainbow Valley in the Northern Territory.

OVERLEAF: Free-standing sandstone cliffs, part of the James Range in Rainbow Valley, glow in the afternoon sun when the rainbow-like rock bands are highlighted.

ABOVE: The Katherine River flows below the towering, brilliantly coloured walls of Katherine Gorge in Nitmiluk National Park

RIGHT: Ochre coloured gorges with their rugged escarpments border Palm Valley in the Finke Gorge National Park. A lush oasis surrounded by harsh desert, Palm Valley is a reminder of when tropical rainforests covered this part of the continent 60 million years ago.

OPPOSITE TOP: The cliffs of Kings Canyon plunge dramatically from the escarpment for about 300 metres into the valley below, forming the Red Centre's deepest gorge.

OPPOSITE BOTTOM RIGHT: Rock-hard termite mounds, constructed of digested mud, dot the landscape in the 'Top End' of the region.

OPPOSITE BOTTOM LEFT: The Wichetty Grub Totem at Emily Gap, one of the many ancient Aboriginal rock carvings found throughout the Northern Territory.

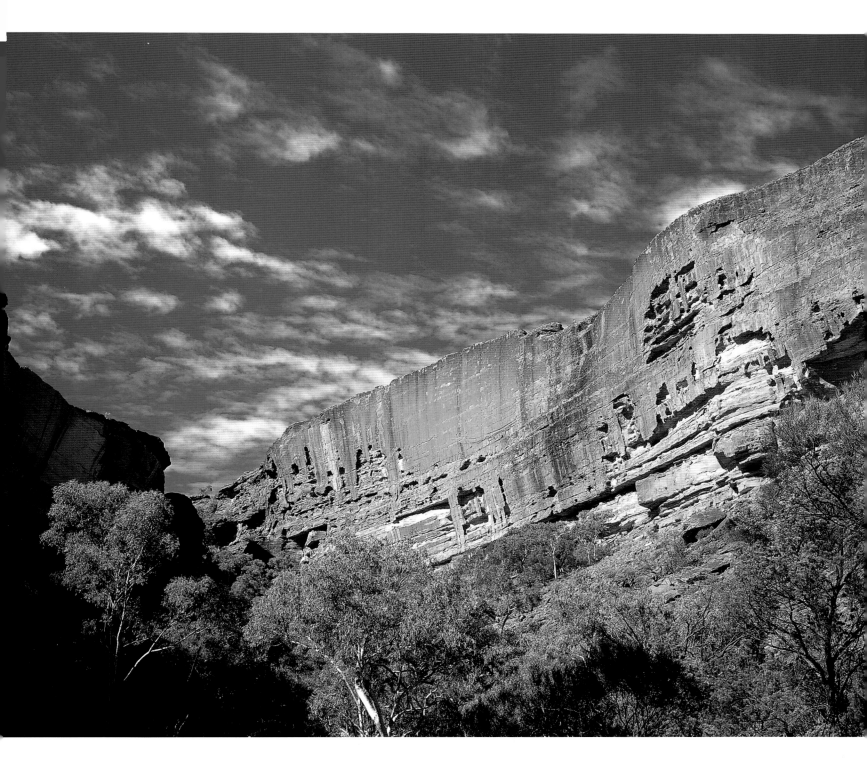

OPPOSITE: Chambers Pillar, at the edge of the Simpson Desert, was used as a landmark by early explorers.

LEFT: Lush vegetation and luke warm water create a tropical resort at the Mataranka Thermal Pool in Elsey National Park.

BELOW: Rivers and creeks have sculpted attractive scenery of rough ranges and red rock, dotted with white-trunked gums in the MacDonnell naturelands.

RIGHT: Every dry season thousands of visitors enjoy boat tours through the majestic scenery of the Katherine River in Katherine Gorge National Park. During the wet season brown flood-waters surge through the gorge.

BELOW: Torrential annual flooding of the Katherine River has cut a mighty gorge through rock plateau leaving ancient sandstone walls towering above the waterway.

OPPOSITE: Dramatic rock formations and sheer red sandstone cliffs in King's Canyon were carved by ancient water-ways.

OVERLEAF:Sunset paints the Devils Marbles a rich red. These weathered, rounded boulders balance precariously on top of one another beside the high-way to Alice Springs, south of Tennant Creek. In Aboriginal mythology, the stones were said to be the eggs of the Rainbow Serpent.

ABOVE: Bizarre rock formations such as Aladdin's Lantern are found throughout Kings Canyon.

RIGHT: The wildly fractured orange and red quartzite walls of Ormiston Gorge are reflected in the clear, still waters of the Finke River.

BELOW: Spectacular red walls tower above the Finke River, one of the oldest watercourses in the world.

OVERLEAF: The jagged, red rock cliffs of Glen Helen Gorge with the flanks of Mt Sonder rising on the horizon.

OPPOSITE: Outback colours at Glen Helen Gorge, west of Alice Springs.

OPPOSITE BOTTOM LEFT: The Ross River flows alongside the East MacDonnell Ranges. Rising abruptly in stark, jagged crests, the great curve of the MacDonnell Ranges make a 400–kilometre wall across the very heart of Australia.

OPPOSITE BOTTOM RIGHT: South Australia meets the Northern Territory.

ABOVE: The prehistoric palms and tranquil rock pools of Palm Valley are a focal point of the Finke Gorge National Park, a wilderness area covering 45 000 hectares west of Alice Springs.

RIGHT: Tortured rock scenery at Elliot, a small town north of Tennant Creek.

ABOVE: Formed from the same terracotta-coloured sandstone as Uluru and Katatjuta, the cliffs of Kings Canyon are extremely prone to erosion by wind and water, creating a range of weathered shapes.

RIGHT: Storm clouds gather over a weather-beaten river gum at Todd River, Alice Springs. The river, which runs through the town, is dry except after flash floods. Each year it is the venue for a 'dry' yacht race, a quirky event in which the competitors run on the bed of the river carrying home-made replicas of harbour yachts.

OPPOSITE TOP: A monument commemorating Aboriginal artist Albert Namatjira stands in the MacDonnell Ranges. Unusually, Albert Namatjira (1902–1959) painted in a traditional European style and his paintings are greatly sought after today.

OPPOSITE BOTTOM RIGHT: Sunrise or sunset is the best time to see the abundant wildlife at the Fogg Dam Sanctuary, east of Darwin.

OPPOSITE BOTTOM LEFT: Road sign at Tennant Creek on the Stuart Highway. This town was rumoured to have been founded when a beer wagon broke down and the drivers stayed to drink the cargo.

Published by
Woollahra Sales and Imports
Unit 6, 32–60 Alice Street, Newtown, New South Wales, 2042, Australia
Telephone: (02) 9557 8299  Fax: (02) 9557 8202
Produced for the publisher by
Murray David Publishing
35 Borgnis Street, Davidson, New South Wales, Australia, 2085

First published 1999
Publishing Director: Murray Child
Marketing Director: David Jenkins
Photographs © Geoff Higgins, 1999, 2004
Text © Murray David Publishing, 1999, 2004
Design © Murray David Publishing, 1999, 2004
Digital film  by Typescan, Adelaide, South Australia
Printed in Indonesia

This revised edition first published 2002
Reprinted 2004


ISBN:  1 876553 00 6

RITORY 191

PICTURES

*Arufura*

*Timor    Sea*

Melville
Island

Bathurst
Island

Kakadu
National Park

**Darwin**  Humpty
Doo

Rum
Jungle

Adelaide
River  Pine
Creek  **ARNHEM**

Border
Store

*West
Alligator*

*East
Alligator R.*

*Liverpool R.*

*Wilson*

*Joseph
Bonaparte
Gulf*

Nitmiluk
(Katherine Gorge)
National Park

*Katherine
R.*

Elsey
National Park

*Daly
River*

*Victoria*

Wyndham

Kununurra

*Lake
Argyle*

Victoria
River
Downs

*Victoria
River*

Daly Waters

*Wickham R.*

*Campfield
R.*

• Elliot

**THE
KIMBERLEYS**

Derby

Geikie Gorge

Purnululu
National Park
(Bungle Bungles)

*Ord
River*

Broome

*King
Sound*

*Fitzroy    River*

Fitzroy
Crossing

Halls Creek

Wave
Hill

Tennant
Creek

*Goss*

**NORTHE**

GREAT    SANDY    DESERT

• Rabbit Flat

*Hansen
R.*

Devils
Marble

Port Headland

*De Grey*

PINNACLE
DESERT

Marble Bar

• The Granites

**TERRITO**

Dampier

Barrow Island

Roebourne

*Yule
River*

Wittenoom

*River*

Yuendumu

*Fortesque River*

North West Cape
Exmouth

Onslow

**THE
PILBARA**

**HAMERSLEY RANGE**

Glen Helen

Ormiston
Gorge

*MACDONNELL    RANGES*

Cape Range
National Park

Tom Price

Karijini National Park

*Lake
Disappointment*

GIBSON    DESERT

Finke Gorge
National Park

**Alice
Springs**

*INDIAN*

*Ashburton*

Newman

• Kings
Canyon

Rainb
Valley
Cons.

Winning Pool

Mount
Vernon

*River*

Mundiwindi

**WESTERN**

*PETERMANN RANGES*

Giles

Uluru-Katatjuta
National Park

Kennedy Range
National Park

Pt. Quobba

*Gascoyne    River*

Milgun

*MUSGRAVE    RANGES*

*The    Alberga*

Carnarvon

*Wooramel    River*

*Shark Bay*

*River*

Meekatharra

• Wiluna

**AUSTRALIA**

GREAT    VICTORIA    DESERT

Marla

**SOUTH**

*OCEAN*

*Dirk Hartog Island*

Denham

Cue

*Murchison    River*

**AUSTRAL**

Kalbarri
National Park

Kalbarri

*Greenough River*

Sandstone

Mount
Magnet

Leonora

*Lake
Barlee*

Stuart Cr

Yalgoo

Ooldea

• C

**Geraldton**

Dongara

Carnamah

*Lake
Moore*

Bonnie Rock

Forrest

Mullewa

**Kalgoorlie**

Coolgardie  **Boulder**

Zanthus

**NULLARBOR    PLAIN**

Nullarbor

Southern Cross

Eucla

Penong

Ceduna

Nambung National Park

*Moore
River*

Moora

**Perth**

*Swan
River*

Northam

York

Hyden

Norseman

Balladonia

Eyre

Streaky Bay

Rottnest Island
Fremantle

Pinjarra

Lake King

Salmon Gums

Bunbury

Collie

Pingrup

Esperance

*Great    Australian    Bight*

Port Li

Cape Leeuwin-
Naturaliste National Park

Augusta

Katanning

Hopetoun

Normalup
Denmark  **Albany**

*King George Sound*

Flinders Chase Na